red e̶... love

red eye

A comedy by

arnold weinstein

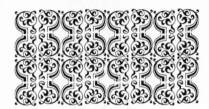

# of love

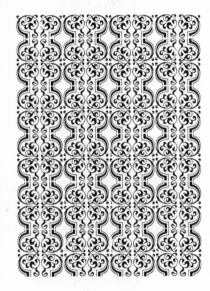

Grove Press, Inc., New York

Evergreen Books Ltd., London

For Jane

and my parents

notes on production

RED EYE OF LOVE was presented at The Living Theatre in New York on June 12, 1961 by Sam Cohn, John Wulp, and Julia Miles. It was directed and designed by Mr. Wulp, with incidental score by William Bolcom, costumes by Willa Kim, and lighting by Nicola Cernovich. The cast was as follows:

WILMER FLANGE, *a poor young fool*	George Latchford
O. O. MARTINAS, *richer, older*	Michael Vale
SELMA CHARGESSE, *a loving young thing*	Jane Romano
FIRST POLICEMAN, *a music lover*	Al Mancini
SECOND POLICEMAN, *a people hater*	Jim Gormley
CAB DRIVER	Barry Primus
WOMAN	Sarah Braveman
VENDOR	Jerry DeLuise
NEWSBOY	Benjamin Hayeem
FRANCES	K. C. Townsend
WAITRESS	Julia Miles
YOUNG BEZ, *six years old* (*to be played by a child*)	Gregory Deutsch
SCRUB LADY	Sarah Braveman
NIGHT WATCHMAN	Robb Grace
TOUGH	Barry Primus
BIG BEZ, *twelve years old* (*to be played by an adult*)	Benjamin Hayeem
ALUM	Barry Primus
UNCLE SAM	Jerry DeLuise

FIRST SOLDIER	John Weston
SECOND SOLDIER	Robb Grace
THIRD SOLDIER	Jim Tiroff
ENEMY SOLDIER	Benjamin Hayeem
A BOY	Gregory Deutsch
WOMAN, *his mother*	Sarah Braveman
THE MIMES (HIGH HAT ROBBER *and* VICTIM)	Robert World and Martha Shaw

MOURNERS, PASSERS-BY

(Most of the minor roles are interchangeable. The play takes place over a period of many years. Some of the characters age, some do not.)

NOTE: The New York production was extremely simple, utilizing as few props and as little furniture as possible. Future productions may be as simple or as lavish as the individual directors and designers desire.

In the New York production, projections were flashed on the front curtain prior to the beginning of several scenes. Future productions may use projections, sign boards carried onstage by actors and placed Stage Left as in the days of vaudeville, or dispense with either at their option.

The author wishes to acknowledge the assistance of John Wulp, Audrey Wood, Jeannette Hirsch, and James Bohan.

Photographs from the New York production by John Wulp

act one

SCENE ONE

"The Beginning: In which it all begins."

A street. A spotlight reveals a girl, SELMA CHARGESSE, *dancing. People pass by without noticing her. Then another spotlight goes on and reveals a shoeshine man,* O. O. MARTINAS, *sitting in a shoeshine chair and staring in the direction of the girl, seemingly transfixed by her dancing. Later we discover that he is actually watching the thirteen-story department store directly behind her. Enter* NEWS-BOY, VENDOR, CAB DRIVER, *and* WOMAN. WILMER *enters, watches people pass girl by, turns to admire girl, then speaks to* MARTINAS, *who gets out of the shoeshine chair.* WILMER *sits down in the chair and* MARTINAS *begins to shine his shoes.*

WILMER: Answer: What would the world do without our type of people, people who stop to watch a girl dance in the street like this?

MARTINAS: Like what?

WILMER: Can't you see her arms and legs moving the daylight this way and that?

MARTINAS: By God! Why didn't anyone tell me she was dancing there? Look at her legs moving the daylight this way and that.

WILMER: Couldn't you see her before?

MARTINAS: See who?

WILMER: The girl dancing there.

MARTINAS: What girl? I was looking at that beautiful department store which will one day be the O. O. Martinas Department Store, named after O. O. Martinas. Who's O. O. Martinas? I'm O. O. Martinas. Who did you think he was? And I was?

WILMER: That silver and stucco thirteen-story building will be yours? Because your name is O. O. Martinas?

Girl stops dancing.

MARTINAS: Yes and no. Yes, the building will be mine becount of my name is O. O. Martinas; becount of when O. O. Martinas wants something, it will be his. I wanted this shoeshine job. It's now mine.

WILMER: That's yes. What's no?

MARTINAS: No, don't you stick your nose into my affairs.

Girl exits.

MARTINAS (*trying to regain* WILMER'S *attention*): My building will be my department store!

WILMER: How does one come by a thirteen-story department store?

MARTINAS: It's simple. You get in on the ground floor. You buy a delicatessen concession—on the ground floor—and before you know it, it's a delicatessen department. Just think! A whole floor of nothing but meat.

WILMER: Meat?

MARTINAS: Yes, I'm a man who believes in meat. Anything on the hoof! I wouldn't shine your shoes unless they were made of cowhide. I hate those who eat innocent vegetables and fruits. Have you ever seen a lettuce pluck a man?

WILMER: A delicatessen department?

MARTINAS: Yes, you young fool. I'll revolutionize department storedom! What this country needs is a revolution. Today, a delicatessen concession, tomorrow, the whole store—

WILMER (*interrupting*): Is that your key?

MARTINAS: Key? What's *that*?

WILMER: You mean you open up a thirteen-story department store and it's not your key to the universe?

MARTINAS: We will have livers, all kinds of livers. Have you ever heard of whooping crane livers? No, you young fool, what do *you* know about the liver field?

Girl starts dancing by. WILMER, *frightened, turns to the girl.*

(MARTINAS *immediately becomes pleasant. Taking out a piece of paper.*) A poem—mine! (*Declaims.*)

> Tinkle, tinkle, little life,
> how I wish I had a wife.
> Deep within my soul so blue
> how come you do me like you do?

Do you like my beautiful words? (*Hands* WILMER *the paper which is painted black.*) Of course there's nothing on it, young fool! Why should there be? I cannot read. Nor write. But I can count! Grant me that! Please grant me that. I can count, becount of. . . . Look: 1, 2, 3, 4, 5, 6, 7, 8, 9, 10, 11, 12, 13! and a half, if you consider the basement, which I consider. It will be mine. The venison, mine; the pig snouts, the bunnies, the tails of oxen, mine; mine the men and women, the heads and guts of all forms of the animal kingdom, mine. All this talk makes me thirsty. Mine! I could use a nice refreshing glass of blood. Mine!

NEWSBOY (*turns and sees dancing girl*): Hey, everyone! A girl dancing!

MARTINAS: Of course. Where?

CAB DRIVER (*who had seen her and paid no attention*): By God, the boy here is right!

Other passers-by now begin to notice her as a crowd gathers. She is inspired.

NEWSBOY: Her hands, she's using hands!

CAB DRIVER: My God! Her leg is moving!

WOMAN: Waving of the arms!

VENDOR: Slow spinning, did you ever . . . ?

WILMER: I don't dance. Strange, my mother was a good dancer, very fat but a good dancer.

CAB DRIVER: They say the fat are light on their feet.

VENDOR: Let me see. Don't hog.

MARTINAS: I'll sell whole hog and loin of yak.

WILMER: It's like watching a baby's dream. I've never seen anyone dance in this street.

MARTINAS: I've never seen anyone dance in *any* street. You don't acquire delicatessen departments watching people dance in the street. I will sell hearts! I will hold thousands of hearts in these hands of mine!

WILMER: I had a friend named Cohn, used to dance—with his face. He used to grin and your eyes would wiggle.

VENDOR: I'd like to see her dance barefoot at my house. Naked!

MARTINAS: Are you an artist?

VENDOR: No, I'm well off, I have a very expensive rug. Nobody's ever danced on that rug. Naked! I can't leave, although I have important appointments up-town. I'm in neckties.

MARTINAS: I never wear ties: I believe in freedom of the neck.

Two policemen come on the scene from opposite side.

FIRST POLICEMAN: Break it up. Break what up?

SECOND POLICEMAN: O.K., O.K.

FIRST POLICEMAN (*to* SECOND POLICEMAN): Are you new on this beat? Can we be partners?

SECOND POLICEMAN: We've got to get her out of here.

MARTINAS: Efficient police. The world is good to me. Thank God, I deserve it. Beautiful girl. Take her away becount of she's blocking the entrance to the future O. O. Martinas Department Store.

FIRST POLICEMAN: Lady, you're disturbing the peace of the entrance to the future O. O. Martinas Department Store.

WILMER: Officer, mind if I told you something? It's nothing personal. It's about your life.

SECOND POLICEMAN *approaches menacingly.*

MARTINAS: Let the boy rave on.

WILMER: Thank you. That girl *has* to dance, just as you have to stop her from dancing. (*To* SECOND POLICE-MAN.) Just as you (*Affectionately puts arm on shoulder of cop.*) have to punch people in the guts and be an officer of the law, just as Martinas here wants to own meats and dollars and peoples. Just as I, just as I —I don't know. I don't know what I have to do. I have no key to the universe. No. Not. So let her dance.

MARTINAS: Who?

Girl starts dancing in appreciation.

SECOND POLICEMAN *is terrified: he doesn't know what to do. He turns on* WILMER *roughly with his club.*

WILMER *runs off and makes a ballet leap into the wings. A crash of garbage cans is heard off-stage.*

FIRST POLICEMAN *has been watching dancinig girl. The* SECOND POLICEMAN *slyly takes the girl, still dancing, and is slyly about to escort her in the direction of the patrol car, when* FIRST POLICEMAN *gently, as her dancing slows down, takes her arm and waves toward stage left.*

FIRST POLICEMAN: Cabbie!

WILMER (*re-enters holding his head*): Dancing girl, if ever you need me. I'll be waiting. Here. (*Reaches into pocket, finds no money.*) I'll get a job!

SECOND POLICEMAN *threatens him.* WILMER *exits into wings with garbage can crash.*

FIRST POLICEMAN (*to* CAB DRIVER): Here! Five dollars. Take her where she wants. Keep the change. Don't look so sneaky suspicious. I'm the law. I arrest. Stop staring!

CAB DRIVER: And I wanted to be a priest!

CAB DRIVER *and girl leave. Sound of cab leaving.* SECOND POLICEMAN *slyly watches the* FIRST POLICEMAN. *They walk off together.*

FIRST POLICEMAN (*apologetic, to* SECOND POLICEMAN): I like rhythm. I like you. Let's be partners! Let's forever walk this beat together—ever!

SECOND POLICEMAN (*slyly and disdainfully staring*): Yes.

WILMER (*enter bedraggled*): You still have another shoe of mine to shine.

MARTINAS: I've given up the shining of shoes. I must make real money. I'm going into butcher delivery. I can see it now.

WILMER: The delicatessen department?

MARTINAS: The delivery list!

Blackout.

SCENE TWO

PROJECTION ON CURTAIN

"Years Later"

A street. The FIRST POLICEMAN *is conducting traffic in front of the curtain. He pretends he is leading a symphony orchestra. He is carried away, about to reach a magnifi-cent crescendo when the* SECOND POLICEMAN *blows his whistle and stops it all.*

SECOND POLICEMAN: O.K., O.K., break it up.

FIRST POLICEMAN: Break what up? I'm one of you. Hey, shine my shoes.

SECOND POLICEMAN: It would be cheating. Policemen have to police, not shine shoes. I hate cops cheating.

FIRST POLICEMAN: I like the slapping on leather. I love music. I love rhythm.

A holdup occurs directly behind them. This is the HIGH HAT ROBBER *who tiptoes up to the woman* VICTIM *and steals her purse. The two policemen are facing front and do not see it.*

SECOND POLICEMAN: Look! We've got no time for music.

HIGH HAT ROBBER *and* VICTIM *leave.*

We've got to guard the O. O. Martinas Emporium. What a revolution in department storedom. It's an honor to guard those genuine thirteen stories.

FIRST POLICEMAN: It's an honor to conduct—traffic. (*Starts conducting his symphony of cars again. Again the* SECOND POLICEMAN's *whistle stops him.*) My cars . . .

SECOND POLICEMAN: Cars! Let 'em drop dead! Long live genuine department stores!

FIRST POLICEMAN: Long live genuine America! Accept no substitutes.

They exit through the following park scene.

SCENE THREE

*A park. A park bench with a single tree standing nearby.
Lights come back up to reveal* o. o. martinas, *who looks
the same.* wilmer *enters, he has aged.*

martinas: Good late afternoon.

wilmer: Good late afternoon.

martinas: Have we met before?

wilmer: No. You look familiar, and since I always forget
a face and never remember a name, we cannot have
met.

martinas: O. O. Martinas is the name. How do you do,
young man?

wilmer: I'm old. I'm twenty-five.

martinas: Yes, sneaks up on you, old age. Hits before
you're ready and you're old before you're ready. Life
is always one step ahead of you. You get ready to be
a child when Bong! Adolescence hits you. Begin to
put up with adolescence and Bong! You're an adult.
Finally realize you're an adult. Plop! Middle age.
And you only believe you're really middle-aged
when Plop! Old age comes limping by and grabs
your bony hand. On your death bed, as you laugh
your last sob, finally you say "Plop bong! I'm old!"
But too late, you're dead. But you've finally caught
up. You're dead and you *know* you're double plop
double bong dead.

wilmer (*disgusted*): Very nice.

martinas: Not bad for teatime. You should hear me in

the office. Eloquent, mystical—

WILMER *is staring out at something.*

Do you like that department store?

WILMER: I was not looking at the department store. I was looking at that girl going in it.

MARTINAS: That's my love.

WILMER: She's a little young.

MARTINAS: The *building* is my love. I own it. Thirteen floors of department store.

WILMER: What's your favorite department?

MARTINAS: Lamb! It's a meat department store. Thirteen floors of meat—nothing else.

WILMER: Do you need a bookkeeper?

MARTINAS: Not only do I own that building, I bought a foreign English bicycle.

WILMER: Do you own a good bookkeeper?

MARTINAS: Would you believe I worked my way up from delivering Italian salami? I used to sit staring with envy at everyone: now I sit staring at my building, my love. First floor, loins of beef; second floor, veal; third floor, lamb! fourth floor, me, a large apartment, right behind the chopping room. Do I sleep!

WILMER *is making a horrible grimace.*

What are you doing with your face? Smile! People like to see the bookkeeper smile.

WILMER: I'm smiling. Can't you read my eyes?

MARTINAS: I can't read. A lovely meat department store

and I can't read or write! Thing I love about me is, I never stop being amazed by my achievements. Do me a favor? Write down the following:

WILMER *pulls a pencil and a roll of adding-machine paper from his pocket.*

I'm in the mood for building poetry. (*Recites the poem.*)

> Death, you old schoolteacher,
> don't take away your books,
> death, you old schoolteacher
> don't ask me to die.
> Death, you old professor,
> I don't want to graduate.
> I want to wear a cap and gown and sock
> you in the eye.
> You big fat witch, death, you.

WILMER: You do this to bookkeepers? I refuse the job.

MARTINAS: I can count too! May not know how to read, know how to count. That's why I own meats and monies.

WILMER: Bookkeeping: key to the universe.

MARTINAS: Money: key to the bank.

WILMER: Can a man die happy without a key to the universe?

MARTINAS: Can a man die happy with one? Don't talk about death. Read my poem about death.

WILMER: No.

MARTINAS (*hurt*): I've got to go: my meat building needs me. You're making that awful face again! Stop!

WILMER: I'm smiling. I'm on vacation.

MARTINAS: Prove it.

WILMER: I went to a party yesterday.

MARTINAS: Why wasn't I invited? Who gave it? Your dad? Your dear old mom?

WILMER: No one I know. I saw a group of people and followed them to a party.

MARTINAS: I cater to the best parties.

WILMER: Then a terrible thing. I went to the bathroom and was very impressed with the odor of soap, perfume, bath oil, underarm deodorant, shaving cream, and toothpaste in the new press-down container.

MARTINAS: I like a good smell.

WILMER: I took hair tonic, gave myself a good brushing and rejoined the festivities. The hostess said, "Pooh! what a smell." The host said, "Yes dear." I went back to the bathroom and took a shave, put on more hair tonic, after-shave lotion, underarm deodorant, for revenge.

MARTINAS: Well done.

WILMER: Then took a shower to get rid of the smell. A, I did not need their scent. B, I was ashamed of myself. Is that stealing?

MARTINAS: My boy, time, which is forever being born and forever dying, has no time for distinctions. What kind of a party was it?

WILMER: A funeral party. That group of people was outside a funeral parlor. I had nothing to do and they were all hugging, chatting, waving, meeting relatives for the first time, vowing to see more of one another, looking at the time, trying not to talk business, or do business, they looked so cheerful and inviting that I couldn't resist following the crowd to the coffin. When I wept over the body they thought I was a long-lost lover of the deceased, a woman of sixty with beautiful blue hair. *They* invited me to the party afterwards. Was I moved. Vacations are *lonely!* The food was good.

MARTINAS: I cater to the best funeral parties. Goombye!

Exit MARTINAS.

WILMER *watches a group of* mourners *behind a coffin. He is about to join them when they follow an ice-cream* VENDOR *and his cart. They exit.*

Enter the dancing girl, SELMA, *aged somewhat. She sits down on the bench.* WILMER *looks at her. She looks at him. They like each other.* WILMER *does not know what to do. He decides. He stands up, looks determinedly toward her and walks to ice-cream* VENDOR, *who has just re-entered.*

WILMER: Two ice creams. One pistachio and one pistachio.

VENDOR: No pistachio and no pistachio. (*Digs into cart and comes up with:*) A tuna fish sandwich.

WILMER: Cut in half?

VENDOR: Yes.

VENDOR *gives him sandwich.* WILMER *pays with a bill.*

(*Angrily.*) A hundred dollar bill is the smallest you have?

WILMER: I'm on vacation.

VENDOR: Nobody makes a fool of me and gets away with it! Except God. I'll show you.

Drops bag of change on WILMER's *toe.*

WILMER: All pennies? No, there's one nickel shining through it all.

VENDOR: You deserve it.

Puts bill in his pocket. Exits.

WILMER *goes to* SELMA, *gives her half a sandwich, sits beside her, and they eat in silence on the bench.*

SELMA: Let's not tell each other our names. It's more romantic.

WILMER: I believe in no names. Makes forgetting much more beautiful.

They eat in silence.

I'm on vacation, spending it in the city.

SELMA: Where do you live?

WILMER: In the city. Up there in my bookkeeping office. You live in the city year in, year out, and forget what sights there are. I have two weeks off, each day to a place I haven't seen in years. Old Cohn and I always went to a museum of natural art or some place. Now, I like my job, but getting up in the morning, going to work, coming home, the result is you don't go anywhere else because you're just nervous. You're tangled, you're twisted, and the result is you think that going anywhere is going to work. Morning becomes night, week becomes weekend, yesterday becomes today. Whatever's happened has not had time to matter. The result is I spend my vacation in the city going places, trying to catch up. The result is I've seen twelve movies in three days.

SELMA: When you look through leaves, the universe looks green.

WILMER: The key!?

SELMA: The key to the green universe?

WILMER: What is it? I know you know. Bookkeeping, right?

SELMA: Movies.

WILMER (*sad*): I knew she knew.

SELMA: It's the only way out.

WILMER: The only?

SELMA: In the movies, no world falls on you.

WILMER: Yes, no world!

They look at each other and kiss.

SELMA (*breaks from the embrace suddenly*): What movies?

WILMER (*still reacting to the kiss*): "Alexander the Great."

SELMA: Saw it.

WILMER: "The Good Earth."

SELMA: Saw it.

WILMER: "The Ten Commandments."

SELMA: Saw them.

WILMER: The key!

SELMA: I *think* I saw it.

WILMER: No. Movies as key to the universe. Along with bookkeeping. Not that I want to take any glory and responsibility away from movies.

SELMA: Are you a bookkeeper?

WILMER: Yes.

SELMA: Exactly. Bookkeeping is the other key to the universe.

WILMER: Say that again!

SELMA: Bookkeeping: other key to universe.

WILMER *stares, moved to tears. He forces himself to speak.*

WILMER: Why are *you* so lonely?

SELMA: Did I say I was lonely?

WILMER: Yes.

SELMA: That's a lie, but I *am* lonely.

She is staring in the direction of Martinas building.

WILMER: I was staring at that building before, but you were in front of it. Why are you staring at it? Is it yours too?

SELMA: No, but it will be. I'm engaged to the owner, O. O. Martinas. We're to be married soon. A week or two or three years.

WILMER (*screams at the top of his voice*): Lonely!! (*Pause.*) Old Cohn, crazy fool, last night married some girl who had eyes that went all the way *in*, dark. *Dark* dark. I was invited to the wedding. I don't drink: just last night a few; I kept eating not to get sick from the booze. (*Pause.*) I got sick from the eating. (*Pause.*) This morning I got sick from the booze. I bit his bride when I was drunk. Old Cohn laughed. (*He laughs.*) I fail to see what's funny.

SELMA: Who is Old Cohn?

WILMER: Old Cohn. My best friend till the eighth grade. We used to go everywhere together and he used to make faces and sing on top of the open-air bus. We lost touch.

SELMA: Lost touch. *You* talk about lost touch! I've lost such touch! I never go to sleep without thinking of Geraldine, the greatest friend you'd ever want to find in the fourth grade. We used to walk through the streets for hours identifying automobiles. We saw them all; we could guess the year from two blocks away. And you talk about losing touch! I can't bear it.

WILMER: Did she die?

SELMA: She moved out of the neighborhood. At the very wrongest time. We had seen all the cars, except one: the Lincoln Zephyr. It was our dream to see in person the Lincoln Zephyr zooming down the street. I saw it two days after she moved away. I didn't know where she lived: Her father must have got poorer or richer; they didn't let anyone know where they went. And here I was, completely unable to let Geraldine know I had seen the Lincoln Zephyr. I'm haunted with that. I think her name was Geraldine.

WILMER: Today I tried singing on top of the open-air bus

like Old Cohn, there in the open, the wind and noise all around. I always turned red, *red* red, made believe I didn't know him. "Stop making fools of the two of us," I'd yell, yell because of the wind and noise all around. Embarrassed me to death, making funny faces to all the city, singing at the top of his voice on top of the open-air bus.

SELMA: Today *you* wanted to sing. I once wanted to dance to all the city. And I did. Look what it got me. Money and wealth.

WILMER: I couldn't sing today.

SELMA: Why?

WILMER: No more open-air buses.

SELMA: Why?

WILMER: I don't remember any songs.

SELMA: Everywhere you turn—a wall.

WILMER: I can hum. (*He hums two notes, then stops.*) No, I can't. There were boys—Cohn was one—could memorize anything. "The Declaration of Independence," "Friends, Romans, Countrymen—," "Stardust," anything. Where did it get them? I took up bookkeeping, guess what I became. A bookkeeper. Those boys memorizing, what do they become? Memorizers? Heasly, seventh grade, won the elocution prize; sells lawn furniture in the A & P. My motto is let people do what they want. Only, take up something that can be the key. Bookkeeping's no drudgery either, it's interesting, responsible too. Think of the chaos the world would be in today if we had no bookkeeping. (*Pause.*) Why is book-keeping not the key?

SELMA: Soft people interest me. I like you.

WILMER: Do you love me? That's important too!

SELMA: As a matter of fact, I do.

WILMER: What about Mr. Martinas?

SELMA: Was he here? O. O. was here?

WILMER: Yes.

SELMA: O. O. and I, we don't get along.

WILMER: Why are you going to marry him?

SELMA: Was I going to marry him? I *was* going to marry him, I guess. But O. O. and I don't get along and I love you.

WILMER: This is the thing, I don't go around breaking up love affairs.

SELMA (*she extends her hand*): Shake. I'm the same way. (*Kisses him passionately as they shake hands.*) I don't like O. O. Him forever talking about his accomplishments, owner of thirteen stories of store. So what, I ask you, so what?

WILMER (*joyfully*): Yes, so what!

SELMA: So it's my duty to marry money. He can be very kind.

WILMER: I suppose.

SELMA: He can be very cruel.

Shows WILMER *her arm.*

WILMER: I don't see anything.

SELMA: Yes, well, anyway, O. O. and I, we just don't hit it off, in any manner or form, if you know what I mean.

WILMER: You mean—

SELMA: In any manner or form. I mean—

WILMER: In any manner or form. We mean—

BOTH: In any manner or form.

SELMA: The result is, I pick you. You're nice, soft: you know I like that. I'm blunt.

WILMER (*growing more and more elated*): Yes!

SELMA: You be blunt.

WILMER: Yes! Yes!

SELMA: If you don't like the idea, get up and walk away.

WILMER: No! No!

SELMA: Fast get up and walk away. I see you hate me, you think I'm a terrible person. Go, I don't blame you, you're nice, you're soft.

WILMER: I cry in the movies.

Romantic music is heard.

SELMA: You cry in the movies? (*She kisses him.*) What movies?

WILMER: "Autumn Leaves."

SELMA: Saw it.

WILMER: "Rhapsody," starring Elizabeth Taylor.

SELMA: Saw it.

WILMER: Cowboy films.

SELMA: You cry in cowboy films?

WILMER: Yes.

SELMA: Which cowboy films?

WILMER: All cowboy films.

SELMA: Saw them.

> *They kiss long. Music stops.*

WILMER: You feel soft to *me*.

SELMA: My name is Selma Chargesse.

WILMER: My name is Wilmer Flange. But you said no names.

SELMA: Names, now that we're in love . . . names.

WILMER (*embracing her*): Not only in love, good friends.

> MARTINAS *enters in a fury.*

MARTINAS: Behind the back! Why is it always behind the back?

WILMER: Sit down, O. O., we'll talk it over.

MARTINAS: I'll give you a good job as bookkeeper.

WILMER: This is the thing, O. O. The girl here loves me and is a little too young for you. Personally, I don't want to get involved. I'm on vacation. But it's not often you meet someone who's nice and soft and loves you.

MARTINAS: I'll make you my bookkeeper.

> WILMER *shakes his head* "*no.*"

I will put my hand in my pocket and take out green paper with a picture of one of the leading leaders of our nation on it.

WILMER *shakes his head "no."*

SELMA: You're quite a guy, Wilmer.

WILMER: My name isn't Wilmer Flange, it's William Flinge. I lied about my name. I wasn't sure then; now that I've made a sacrifice I know you must be worth it.

SELMA: I am, William, I am!

MARTINAS (*to* WILMER): Glad you can't be bribed: you'll be true to her. Head bookkeeper?

WILMER *shakes his head "no."*

Would you mind leaving us together a minute, Sel?

SELMA: Everyone loves me. (*Exits.*)

MARTINAS (*weeps*): Pity an old man, becount of she's all I have.

WILMER: Would she be happy, O. O.?

MARTINAS: I can buy and sell you! No, forget I said that. We must be kind.

WILMER: Strange how I don't mind anything when someone loves me.

MARTINAS: Forgive an old man, may I extend my heartfelt felicitations?

WILMER: You're crying, O. O.

MARTINAS: Yes, these illiterate eyes. . . . But what did I do? (*Angry.*) An empire! The O. O. Martinas building. I can buy and sell you. Without knowing how to read. An empire of meat I built and mine eyes have never lain in locked embrace with the written word. What have you done with your learning? Stolen my fiancée. Keep your reading, keep your writing. Give me good arithmetic. One plus one equals one and one all alone by itself will forever equal none. Who needs reading and writing! (*He sobs.*)

WILMER: Why are you crying?

MARTINAS: Becount of I can't read or write.

WILMER (*holding* MARTINAS' *quaking shoulders*): There are other things.

MARTINAS (*angry again*): Like money! I can buy and sell you! (*He grabs* WILMER *by the throat.*)

WILMER: What did *I* do? I'm nice and soft and getting killed. On my vacation.

MARTINAS: Come on Sel.

Enter SELMA.

WILMER: Stick with me, Selma.

SELMA: I need O. O.'s apartment.

WILMER: I have a hot plate in my office.

MARTINAS: Sel! To the O. O. Martinas building and have an O. O. Special.

WILMER: Go! Do you want to get me killed? Don't answer. Run away with me. No! Not!

MARTINAS (*simultaneously*): Corned beef, liverwurst, pastrami, Italian salami, turkey and tongue on two nice thick . . .

SELMA: When you're alive . . .

MARTINAS: . . . slices of . . .

SELMA: . . . all you can do is live.

MARTINAS: . . .baloney!

SELMA: Is there any of that Russian dressing left?

MARTINAS: I'm a gentleman and a butcher, am I not?

SELMA: Oh, O. O., O.K.

WILMER: Please Selma!

SELMA: Please what?

WILMER: I don't know.

> MARTINAS *takes* SELMA's *arm as if nothing had happened. They mark time ready to march.*

MARTINAS: Good-by, William Flinge. I'm taking Selma home now. I'd offer you a job as head bookkeeper; the atmosphere would be too tense, don't you think?

SELMA: Good-by, Wilmer Flange, for that's the way I'll always remember you.

WILMER: Good-by, Selma Chargesse, for that's the way I'll always remember you.

MARTINAS: Pardon an old sentimental man, William, may I say something before I go?

WILMER: Sure, O. O.

MARTINAS (*violent*): I'll kill you if you ever see Selma again!

SELMA: You're only doing that because you're jealous, O. O.

WILMER: If ever you need me, Selma, I'll be waiting.

> MARTINAS *marches her away.* WILMER *sits miserable.*

WILMER: If bookkeeping cannot change the human side of existence, can movies? The only way out! The

only key! I'm going to see "Bhowani Junction" star-
ring Ava Gardner and Stewart Granger, with Bill
Travers and Abraham Sofaer, directed by George
Cukor and produced by Pandro S. Berman!

He smiles, then breaks into the awful grimace.

Curtain.

SCENE FOUR

The street again. WILMER *enters from movie, carrying a
bag of money and a box of popcorn. Eats last piece of
popcorn and spits it out.*

WILMER: What a rotten movie!

Enter FIRST POLICEMAN *and a girl* FRANCES.

FIRST POLICEMAN: I love you madly.

FRANCES: You don't even remember my name. It's
Frances.

FIRST POLICEMAN: I love you madly, Frances.

WILMER *smiles the awful grimace.*

FRANCES: Hey, that guy's looking funny at me.

FIRST POLICEMAN *slaps* WILMER.

WILMER: I was smiling because you look so happy. But
hit me. I don't care about anything any more. Hit me!
Hit me! I don't care.

FIRST POLICEMAN *slaps* WILMER *again.*

That's enough! now, I go. Nice of you to chat with

me. I have no one, not even Parents! That's a lie. I have parents. See how miserable I am? Lonely and alone enough to lie.

FIRST POLICEMAN: I ought to lock you up, but I and Gertrude will be late for the concert. Music! Rhythm I love!

They exit.

WILMER: I was only making faces at myself.

Enter VENDOR *with two suitcases.*

VENDOR: Dolls! I'm selling dolls! They laugh, they cry, they do everything but die. Why are *you* crying?

WILMER: I'm laughing, and not for unhappiness. I'm glad Selma Chargesse, a casual acquaintance I happen to love, has left me for security. What meals she can eat! Steaks smothered with lamb chops, liver on the side. I'm glad, happy! (*Starts to leave.*)

VENDOR: Where are you going?

WILMER: To kill myself.

VENDOR: That's no key to the situation.

WILMER: What is?

VENDOR (*snapping open suitcase with stand*): Dolls! They understand. Twenty-five cents, thirty-five cents, five cents.

WILMER: I'll take one.

VENDOR: One what?

WILMER: One suitcase of dolls. How much?

VENDOR (*assessing* WILMER's *moneybag*): How much do you have?

WILMER: One hundred dollars in change.

VENDOR: Sold! I'll give it to you for one hundred dollars—in change.

WILMER (*giving him moneybag*): Are you sure this is the key?

VENDOR (*leaving quickly*): It is for me! (*Exits.*)

WILMER (*calls to empty street*): Dolls! I'm selling pretty dolls, dolls that never leave you for another person or another doll. They laugh, they cry, they do everything but die; dolls do not need first cut meats forever down their throats like certain Selma Chargesses. Which reminds me, I'm hungry. Hunger always hunts for misery. (*Sets up suitcase.*) I'm angry, hurt and angry and hungry. Selma, if ever you need me, I'll be waiting. I'm selling dolls that never leave you for another person, or another doll . . . they laugh, they cry, they do everything but die.

Lights fade to blackout.

SCENE FIVE

PROJECTION ON CURTAIN

**"Two Days Later. The O. O. Martinas apartment
in the O. O. Martinas Meat Department Store."**

SELMA *is sitting reading in negligee.* MARTINAS *is on other side of wall in bedroom during entire scene.* SELMA *is reading in an armchair. She dozes, but snaps herself awake and returns to her magazine with a struggle.*

MARTINAS (*in bedroom*): Selma, coming to bed? It's one o'clock. (*Waits. No reaction.*) You're tired too. You worked hard in the cutlet department this morning. (*Waits. No reaction.*) You need sleep. I saw you slaving away in assorted gizzards. (*Waits. No reaction.*) I'm worn out and I can't go to sleep. *It's so lonely in here.*

SELMA: *That's why I don't want to go in there.* (*She is shocked by her own words.*)

MARTINAS: What?

SELMA *is still shocked, but proud.*

What?

SELMA *still does not answer, smiling.*

Were you talking to yourself?

SELMA: Everyone talks to herself sometime or another. Or don't you know that?

MARTINAS: I tell you truly, Selma, I don't.

SELMA: Don't you ever talk to yourself?

MARTINAS: To tell you truly, Selma, I don't. And though I have never truly believed honesty is the best policy, I am speaking truly. Wait! No! I remember, once I spoke to myself.

SELMA: And?

MARTINAS: Nobody listened. I concluded that man doesn't acquire meat department stores by talking to himself; I concluded that meat department stores come to him who talks out loud and says: "World, you old sneak thief, work for me, or I will put you in solitary con-

finement for a long time by committing suicide."
And that's all it takes to be rich, that—and you'll
never guess! Money! Money! Selma, please, come to
sleep becount of my severe case of loneliness.

SELMA *puts coat over her negligee, quietly leaves,
doing her old dance.*

Selma? Are you mad becount of I refuse to talk to
myself?

MARTINAS *enters in pajamas with pork chop pattern.*

Selma. . . . Selma? (*Stares in teary dismay.*)

Lights dim in MARTINAS *apartment.*

SCENE SIX

The street. It is raining.

Lights go up beneath lamppost where WILMER *is selling
his dolls to no one late in the night, his suitcase open.*
SELMA *enters.* WILMER *does not see her.*

WILMER: Dolls that never leave you for another person or
   another doll.

SELMA: Can you believe who is back?

WILMER (*without turning to her*): Selma Chargesse, my
   former casual acqaintance and sweetheart?

SELMA: Right the first time.

   Several people with umbrellas pass between them.

WILMER: Selma. Why did you leave me two days ago for
   the sake of dollars?

SELMA: I only did it for the money.

WILMER: Why did you go off with a man much less your type than my type?

SELMA: Can you forgive me?

WILMER: No, but I will.

SELMA: Oh, William.

WILMER: I've changed my name to Wilmer Flange, officially.

SELMA: Can you change it officially in two days?

WILMER: Two minutes. I looked in the mirror, shouted the national anthem in Greek, Siamese, pig Latin, then whistled the Bill of Rights and bash! Name officially changed from William Flinge to Wilmer Flange.

SELMA: Wilmer, let's go to the movies. Where we belong.

WILMER: Selma, movies are not the key, nor bookkeeping.

SELMA: What is the key?

WILMER (*shows suitcase*): Dolls.

SELMA: Dolls!!? (*Pause as she checks herself.*) You're right.

WILMER: Then promise me one thing.

SELMA: Almost anything! Almost anything!

WILMER: Promise me your next man will be your type and my type.

SELMA: But *you're* more your type and my type than any type.

WILMER: Selma, I got married.

SELMA: Married? You don't want me back! It was a lie, all you said about waiting for me if ever I need you. Two days and you forgot me? Two days?

WILMER: It was more like three, Selma.

SELMA: Two days and three nights.

WILMER: How long can a guy wait? I only married Marguerite for the dolls of it anyway. She owned a doll warehouse.

SELMA: Why, why?

WILMER: For the dolls of it! I needed spare parts for my experiments. I am trying to invent a special doll that sneezes.

SELMA: Good-by. I would wish happiness to you and Marguerite Flange; my heart is not in it mainly because of my extreme love for you. I wish you both a *drop* of joy.

WILMER: Don't forget my son, Bez, a fine boy of one year of age.

SELMA: Married three days—you have a son?

WILMER: Yes, by my wife's husband, *Rocky!*

Music.

SELMA: Good-by, William Flinge, for that's the way I'll always remember you. (*Starts to leave.*)

WILMER: Good-by, Selma Chargesse, for that's the way I'll always remember you. (*Begins to hawk dolls.*) They laugh, they cry, they do everything but die.

SELMA (*stops suddenly*): She had a husband when she married you?

WILMER: Don't worry, she left me yesterday. Said I was obsessed with dolls. Said I never came home. Said I spent all the time inventing dolls. Said the truth.

SELMA: You're a free man, Wilmer! My man! With me you'll be a happy doll inventor.

WILMER: Just what I've always wanted since yesterday.

A baby cries. WILMER *takes a baby from suitcase.*

She said I could have Bez, the child; he's grown to love me in these two days.

SELMA: Three days. Let's go home.

WILMER: And get married officially.

SELMA: At home?

WILMER: We'll look into the mirror, shout the national anthem in Greek, Siamese, pig Latin and bash! the marriage will be official. That's how Marguerite and I got married.

SELMA: How will you divorce her?

WILMER: Do the whole ceremony backwards.

SELMA: Is that legal?

WILMER: Not only legal, religious! Come on, Selma, let's make me a very happy doll inventor. One of my dolls already has a runny nose.

SELMA *sighs with admiration as they march toward* WILMER's *house.*

Curtain.

SCENE SEVEN

PROJECTION ON CURTAIN

**"Years later. The Street. The Night.
The Depression."**

*Street, late at night, years later, near shoeshine stand.
The policemen have aged.*

FIRST POLICEMAN: I hate when the country is in a depression; poor Wilmer and Selma! Together all these years. No money, lack of funds, poverty, second-run movies; shine my shoes.

SECOND POLICEMAN: No!

FIRST POLICEMAN: Don't you want my big boots to glow in the darkness like a bright and beautiful gun? After all, the cows hanging there in O. O.'s window upside down see nothing but shoes.

SECOND POLICEMAN: Cows! Big shots hanging there upside down!

FIRST POLICEMAN: Today they're happy on display with their bellies open, showing how beautiful they are inside; the next day they're gone, forgotten, and new cows take their place in the window, showing off their guts, how bright, how red, one generation to the next.

SECOND POLICEMAN: Cows, hanging there upside down! Let 'em drop dead!

Another robbery occurs behind them. It is the same HIGH HAT ROBBER *and his* VICTIM, *now both a little older.*

Look!

BOTH: Again the late light in Wilmer's doll invention studio, formerly his furnished room, formerly his bookkeeping office.

FIRST POLICEMAN: Wilmer day and night invents new dolls.

SECOND POLICEMAN: Nobody buys them.

FIRST POLICEMAN: After years of failure—

SECOND POLICEMAN: —he finds real failure.

FIRST POLICEMAN: And poor O. O. Martinas.

Enter MARTINAS *who sits at a café table.*

Five new stories added to his meat department store. Two new bone departments. Has money, but you can't get love for money.

SECOND POLICEMAN: Not for love or money.

They exit as:

SCENE EIGHT

MARTINAS *at café table.* WAITRESS *approaches.*

MARTINAS: Uhm, how much for the brandy?

WAITRESS: Seventy cents.

MARTINAS: Uhm, how much for the bourbon?

WAITRESS: Seventy cents. Everything here is seventy cents.

MARTINAS: Uhm, how much for the cognac?

WAITRESS: Listen, are you a wise guy?

MARTINAS: Uhm, how much for you?

WAITRESS (*looks angry, then decides*): Ten dollars.

MARTINAS: Uhm ...

WAITRESS: Ten dollars isn't much. I don't do this for a living. I raise money to send my fifteen-year-old daughter through school. I want her to have the advantages I never had, I want her to be pure.

MARTINAS (*studies the menu a moment then*): Uhm, how much for her?

Blackout.

SCENE NINE

WILMER'S *toy invention studio at night, a tiny room, with boxes, toys, parts of toys in disarray.* WILMER *is sitting behind the desk-worktable, taking the temperature of a doll, feeling its pulse, using a stethoscope on its chest.*

WILMER *looks tired, older.*

SELMA *walks in, carrying a suitcase.* BEZ (*in a sailor suit*), *their six-year-old son, follows. During the scene,* BEZ *keeps hitting* WILMER *with a rubber glove. No reaction from* WILMER.

WILMER: Hello, Selma, hello, Bez, my son. Look at this doll, Bez.

They look at doll.

Does he look sad enough to make people happy? Oh,

if I could only make a doll that dies: five years of walking and jumping, then the little doll gets sick and dies, slowly, beautifully, a beautiful doll death.

SELMA: Wilmer—

WILMER: We could sell doll coffins, doll tombstones, doll cemeteries. Kids would love that. Real live death to play with.

SELMA: Wilmer—

WILMER: Doll germs! Harmless to children, each doll with little doll symptoms built in. It's the key of keys—the life key. What's the matter, Selma, don't you like the idea? (*Takes temperature of doll.*) 98.6—it should be 101 at least.

SELMA: Wilmer, I'm leaving you, *you know that, don't you?*

WILMER: Be back before the first to handle the book-keeping? You're good at it, *you know that, don't you?* I love you, *you know that, don't you?*

BEZ *hits* WILMER.

SELMA: I'm taking Bez and not coming back, Wilmer, *you know that, don't you?*

WILMER: When I love you, Selma, you mustn't divorce me, *you know that, don't you?*

SELMA: You haven't been home for three days, Wilmer, *you know that, don't you?*

WILMER: It was only two.

SELMA: Two days and three nights.

BEZ *hits* WILMER.

WILMER: One more little old chance?

BEZ *hits* WILMER.

SELMA: You'd be home a week, then back here, again, for-getting Bez, me, yourself—did you eat today? Of course not, *you know that, don't you?*

WILMER: Of course not. I was happy, didn't need food, *you know that, don't you?*

SELMA *takes a sandwich from handbag.*

SELMA: Eat now, or you never will, *you know that, don't you?*

WILMER (*eating*): It's not for myself I spend time here. I develop a doll that shrivels up, wastes away and dies, we have security and securities. We'll spend so much time together you'll throw me out of the house. *You know that, don't you? Hahaha!*

With his mouth full of sandwich he weepingly laughs, chokes, drinks water, spills some on her acci-dentally.

He tries to brush her dress, bends down rubbing the skirt.

SELMA (*hysterically*): Get off your knees!

BEZ *hits* WILMER.

WILMER (*hugs her legs*): Am I so wrong?

SELMA (*weeping*): Not wrong but what can we do? It would be wrong if you changed for my sake. Wrong for both of us, *you know that, don't you?*

BEZ *hits* WILMER.

WILMER: I'll see you downstairs at least, *you know that, don't you?*

BEZ *bursts into tears.*

SELMA: Bez!

BEZ: I don't want to leave my daddy! *You know that, don't you?*

BEZ *hits* WILMER.

WILMER: Go, Bez, our son. Protect Mother.

WILMER *is about to escort* SELMA *out when phone rings.*

Oh, that's Mrs. Harris. It's about some important springs. Springs that will make my dolls sick, Selma.

SELMA: I'll write from my mother's.

WILMER: Try to make Bez understand.

SELMA: Understand what?

WILMER: I don't know—*you know that, don't you?*

Exit SELMA *and* BEZ.

And remember—if ever you need me, I'll be waiting. *You know that—*

Phone rings again. He rushes in to answer it. Too late. Takes doll's temperature and bursts into tears. Door opens and an elegantly dressed lady enters.

SCRUB LADY: Still here?

WILMER: Of course I'm here. I'm not there.

SCRUB LADY: Where?

WILMER: That's what *I'd* like to know.

SCRUB LADY: Go home to your wife and kid, rat! All the time here. Are you crazy or what? (*She takes off her coat.*)

WILMER: What. (*Sudden realization!*) My wife left me. That's why I'm here, not there.

SCRUB LADY: Where? (*She rolls up her sleeves.*)

WILMER: Mop up my tears. (*Works on doll.*)

SCRUB LADY: All the time your hands on doll people. Not at home where good men bring hands. (*She brings in a pail and begins to scrub the floor.*)

WILMER: A man has no right to invent dolls that shrivel up, waste away and die?

SCRUB LADY: Not that I'm a bargain, but I want a man home. Even if we knock each other around.

WILMER *is weeping.*

Hey, what's the matter? Did someone pass away? I hate it. All my friends are red in the eyes because of passing-aways. Everyone passes away nowadays.

WILMER: My wife left me.

SCRUB LADY (*holding his head and liking it*): Ah, you should have told me.

WILMER: I need her the way I need—dolls.

SCRUB LADY: Me, I like a man home.

Phone rings, WILMER *rushes, speaks into it.*

WILMER: Hello Mr. Harris. My wife left me. Life without her is like life without dolls. Mr. Harris—Yes, of course, the springs! Sending them? Mr. Harris— (*Hangs up, obviously cut off. Looks at temperature of doll, shakes his head in disappointment.*)

SCRUB LADY: What's the fun of being sad if you can't turn to your friends?

NIGHT WATCHMAN (*enters, with time clock, drunk*): Oh, still here, huh?

WILMER: I'm here!

NIGHT WATCHMAN: There have been burglaries, but don't worry—I'm making my rounds. Not meaning a drop of harm. Speaking of a drop, do you have any whisky you can lend me till my next time around?

WILMER: I'm not a drinking man. Another thing. Did I drink? No.

NIGHT WATCHMAN: No?

WILMER: Go out with other women? No.

SCRUB LADY: No?

WILMER (*grabs* NIGHT WATCHMAN): Why did she leave me? Answer. Why?

NIGHT WATCHMAN: Please let me go. I've got to take care of this building.

NIGHT WATCHMAN, *frightened, is about to leave when* WILMER *holds him back, imploringly and angrily.*

My heart's not strong. I have this drinking problem based on alcohol.

WILMER (*looks at thermometer in doll*): 98.6! Still no good. I'd settle for a mild 100, just a touch of the flu.

NIGHT WATCHMAN: I'm not a well watchman.

Sound of footsteps. All are terrified.

SCRUB LADY (*screams. They all kneel to pray*): Burglars!

WILMER: Lord, don't let the burglars get me until one of my dolls comes down with a toy disease. I can't go on without the key.

SCRUB LADY: Lord, I'll never ever again.

WILMER: Lord, I will always.

NIGHT WATCHMAN: Lord, could I have a drink?

Door opens and a TOUGH *enters. He carries a violin case. He opens the case as all freeze with fear.* TOUGH *takes out a violin, then a package.*

TOUGH: Mr. Wilmer Flange? I have some springs.

WILMER: A delivery boy comes bearing springs.

NIGHT WATCHMAN: No burglary in his soul.

TOUGH: I'm a music student. I work from six to twelve delivering springs; I don't mind; it doesn't conflict with my real work, house painting. Eight hours a day. This is my violin practice hour, but I'm delivering overtime to buy brushes for a new paint job. My masterpiece. A twelve-room basement flat. The rent is twelve bucks a month, but what a job those guys are doing: twelve thousands dollars in decorating it all up. Twelve different shades of off-beige.

WILMER (*to* TOUGH): But springs make the dolls live and, with luck, die. Springs round out their little personalities. I need springs. The troubled universe needs springs. You're not listening. Nobody listens. Can't you hear me? Are you deaf?

TOUGH: I'm sorry, sir, I can't hear you. I'm deaf.

NIGHT WATCHMAN: What about my problem? I'm sober! (*Hops from table to door.*)

WILMER: I'll give you a drink.

NIGHT WATCHMAN *hops back on table.*

SCRUB LADY: I thought you were not a drinking thing.

WILMER: A man has a right.

NIGHT WATCHMAN: Sheer psychology.

TOUGH: You folks sure do fool around and have fun. My ears are unhappy.

The two policemen enter. FIRST POLICEMAN *sees toy tom-toms.*

FIRST POLICEMAN: Who screamed? What's going on here? Oh, music, rhythm!

SECOND POLICEMAN: O.K., O.K., break it up. Break what up? What's the trouble? Who screamed?

FIRST POLICEMAN (*pointing to toy tom-toms*): May I— you know what?

SECOND POLICEMAN: No.

FIRST POLICEMAN: Please let me do it.

SCRUB LADY: Take me away.

SECOND POLICEMAN: Did you scream?

SCRUB LADY: I'm lonely. Take me away.

WILMER *bursts into tears, sits on the floor, takes sandwich, and eats and weeps.*

FIRST POLICEMAN: I'm going to do it!

SCRUB LADY: Going to marry me?

FIRST POLICEMAN (*takes a toy tom-tom and beats it,* TOUGH *joins in on his violin*): Going to play the toy tom-tom.

FIRST POLICEMAN *and* TOUGH *play a duet for violin and toy tom-tom.* SCRUB LADY *sings along.*

Enter SELMA *and* BEZ. SECOND POLICEMAN *sees them and blows his whistle. Music stops.*

SELMA: I, Bez, all two of us crying at the station while you cavort here and have fun. I first came back to stay. Now I'm going to stay.

WILMER: Stay. I'm eating a sandwich of tears.

SELMA: I can't stand it at my mother's. And it's a long trip.

WILMER: Life, you've come through again! (*Embraces* SELMA.)

SELMA: These ten minutes seemed like a quarter of an hour!

WILMER (*rushes to* TOUGH *and shakes him*): Give springs! My little dolls are dying to die; to shrivel up, to waste away, and die. They don't want to be left out. They want to be the key. The key! The springs! The springs! (*Searches* TOUGH. TOUGH *points to table.* WILMER *takes spring and picks up a doll.*)

SELMA: Could Bez and I have a kiss and a dollar fifty to pay the cab?

SCRUB LADY: He's busy! Think of someone but yourself! You all the time want nothing but a man home. Here's quite a guy changing the world of toys!

WILMER: In all fairness, Selma, the lady on my left is right.

BEZ: Who can I hit? Who can I hit?

WILMER keeps working, too absorbed to listen; he is a scientist probing the unknown, a surgeon. Drum roll from FIRST POLICEMAN'S *tom-tom.*

WILMER: Scissors.

SCRUB LADY gives scissors.

Glue.

SCRUB LADY gives glue.

Spring.

BEZ: You're not glad I'm back. I'm taking mother away.

WILMER: This is it! Thermometer.

SCRUB LADY: Here you are, darling.

As WILMER *concentrates, he does not notice* SELMA *writing a note. She and* BEZ *quietly march off, just as* WILMER *inserts thermometer in doll's mouth. He turns to where he thinks* SELMA *is standing.*

WILMER: A whole chapter in the encyclopedia of dolls will be devoted to us in this room on this day.

The two policemen stand at attention.

Selma—(*Sees she has left.*) SELMA!! (*Picks up note, reads aloud.*) "If ever you need me. I'll be waiting. Love, Selma Chargesse, former casual acquaintance and mother of your former wife's son, Bez." (*Pause.*) Darn it! My wife and child have left me again! (*Takes out stethoscope and puts it on doll's chest hopefully.*)

Sound of feet. Everyone in the room is frightened

again. They huddle together: they await their doom.
The door opens, in walks O. O. MARTINAS, *unchanged*
by years.

MARTINAS (*to* WILMER): Forgive an old fool, but haven't
I seen you somewhere before? Give me Selma, to take
away to a more attractive, permissive and lucrative
life: if you know what those words mean you'll hand
her over.

WILMER: I don't know what the words mean, I know
what *you* mean. You can't have her. She's mine. I
wouldn't give her away for all the dolls in China. She
loves me. She left me.

MARTINAS: Then she must be at my house, loving me.

WILMER: She's at her mother's house not loving *her*.

MARTINAS: Her mother died when Selma was a girl of
thirty-one.

WILMER: That's right! She must be at your house.

OTHERS (*conducted by* FIRST POLICEMAN): OOOH.

MARTINAS: How do you think you lived all these years?
My meat department store, twenty-five floors. I sent
you free meat. Becount of her.

OTHERS: OOOH.

WILMER: Disgusting!

MARTINAS (*violent*): What's wrong with my meat? I sent
the second best cuts!

OTHERS: OH?

MARTINAS: Here I kept him in oxtails and entrails!

OTHERS: ECH!

MARTINAS: But the second best!

OTHERS: OH?

MARTINAS: Yet he scorns me and won't give me his wife I deserve. I demand respect.

WILMER: And my dear son, Bez!

MARTINAS: All right, I'll take him too.

OTHERS: AH.

WILMER: Go. I don't need anyone! Dolls will get feverish and die, and make people happy. The Key! The Key! The thermometer.

MARTINAS: I demand respect.

OTHERS: Get respect.

MARTINAS: Goombye! (*Exit.*)

> WILMER *takes thermometer from doll. He looks at thermometer and bows his head in defeat.*

WILMER: 98.6.

OTHERS: OOOOH.

TOUGH: I can't hear them. I'm deaf. *You know that, don't you?*

> *As* WILMER, *crying, eats his sandwich.*

> *Curtain.*

act two

act Two

SCENE ONE

PROJECTION ON CURTAIN

"Years Later. Merry Christmas."

*The dark silent street, empty except for the aging police-
men, counting money.*

FIRST POLICEMAN (*gives* SECOND POLICEMAN *a dollar bill
wrapped in ribbon*): Merry Christmas.

SECOND POLICEMAN (*gives* FIRST POLICEMAN *a dollar bill
in exchange*): Merry Christmas.

FIRST POLICEMAN: Just what I've always wanted—a dollar
bill.

SECOND POLICEMAN: Good times in the nation! Dollar
again buys dollar.

FIRST POLICEMAN: Shine my black shoes with brown
polish? I want to see if nature is indestructible.

SECOND POLICEMAN: It is. Didn't the depression die of
prosperity?

FIRST POLICEMAN: Just let me feel that beat on my feet.

SECOND POLICEMAN: No.

FIRST POLICEMAN: I'm tired of playing ghost and animal
and mineral. André—

SECOND POLICEMAN: Yes?

FIRST POLICEMAN: Can we—? Can we, André?

SECOND POLICEMAN: I knew you'd be getting round to that
sooner or later. No!

FIRST POLICEMAN: We can go on the vacant lot. André, nobody will know.

SECOND POLICEMAN: No!

FIRST POLICEMAN: What's *wrong* with playing cops and robbers?

HIGH HAT ROBBER, *older, robs his* VICTIM *in background.*

BOTH POLICEMEN (*not seeing robbery*): Look!

FIRST POLICEMAN: Again the late light in the O. O. Martinas Meat Mart. Ten new stories added, a used meat department and Selma back in her bloody apron. After years ...

SECOND POLICEMAN: Years. Let 'em drop dead.

FIRST POLICEMAN: Oh, André, don't be that way. If you don't want to play cops and robbers, what do you want to do?

WILMER *enters with suitcase open, hawking.*

WILMER: Dolls!

SECOND POLICEMAN: I know what we can do, let's arrest that bum.

WILMER: Dolls! I'm selling pretty dolls that refuse to get sick, shrivel up and die: and leave you for another person or another doll. One dollar. Christmas is marching on us, Christmas. Can't you taste the snow-drops? Fifty cents.

Policemen walk to him.

FIRST POLICEMAN: Come along with us.

SECOND POLICEMAN: You bum.

WILMER: I'm an enterprising young bum.

SECOND POLICEMAN: You young bum.

WILMER: Merry Christmas.

SECOND POLICEMAN: Merry Christmas, you bum.

FIRST POLICEMAN: Let's give the bum a break.

SECOND POLICEMAN: True. It's Christmas. Peace, good will—(*To* WILMER.) Do you see that sign? Santa Claus needed. Why don't you get a nice position as a saint? You bum.

WILMER: What does a saint do in the O. O. Martinas Meat Mart?

SECOND POLICEMAN: Gives away meat tidbits for tots.

FIRST POLICEMAN: For Christmas' sake! Come along, André.

WILMER *goes to Martinas building.*

Snow will be on the lot covering the dead cars and the building that never got past the framework. It would have been some pretty building, André. The girders were orange! Come along, cops and robbers! If we hurry we'll make dawn.

SECOND POLICEMAN: I get to be the robber.

FIRST POLICEMAN: No! The game's off.

They leave, both furious.

Dawn breaks.

WILMER *at Martinas building looks at sign.* BEZ *enters, and goes toward door. He is grown; wears same sailor suit he wore as little Bez years before.*

BEZ: Excuse me, I live here and work here. Today I help my Dad O. O. choose a Santa. (*Looks in* WILMER'S *suitcase.*) Nice dolls. I'd buy your dolls, but I'm low on cash. My money's tied up in the business.

WILMER (*gives* BEZ *the suitcase*): Take them, all of them.

BEZ (*takes toys*): You should, becount of it's Christmas.

WILMER: I'm going to become a Santa Claus. Would you like to come to the North Pole and live in my apartment?

BEZ: No.

WILMER: You don't want to go into our future family business? What do you want to be when you grow up?

BEZ: A butcher. Becount of I'm a butcher now.

WILMER: Bez, remember me? Your former dad?

BEZ: You're not my former dad. My former dad was a bum. Goombye!

WILMER: Merry Christmas.

Both exit into store.

Lights dim on street and brighten in MARTINAS *office.*

SCENE TWO

MARTINAS *sits at a chopping table-desk. Behind him hangs a huge side of beef as if ready to pounce on him, or hug him.*

MARTINAS (*into intercom*): Professor Alum will be here in ten minutes. Don't disturb me. Professor Alum is a philosopher, philologist, critic, and halfback for Heidelberg in '34. He will give me my first lesson in anything.

Enter a threadbare studious man of forty.

ALUM: Thirty-five floors. Shouldn't you put in elevators?

MARTINAS: Ah, Doctor Professor. Enchanted. Always admired your books. Teach me to read.

ALUM (*picks up three volumes on* MARTINAS' *desk*): Dante, Shelley, Keats? Have you trouble reading Dante, Shelley, and Keats? Is it the symbolism, the metaphor, the syntax?

MARTINAS: The reading. I can't read with my eyes. It's ruining my career as a well-rounded fellow. I'm what cruel people call illiterate.

ALUM: You're a beginner?

MARTINAS: How can you teach enders if you can't teach beginners? Besides, I'm not exactly a beginner: I build poems. May I recite, Doctor Professor? (*Declaims.*)
>   Tho' I lack education,
>   In my estimation
>   There's no other poet
>   Like that Irish poet,
>   Kelly of Kelly and Sheats.

ALUM: What about Dante?

MARTINAS: There's nothing more Dante,
>   Except a lace pantie,
>   Than reading the poems of,

> Those Irish poems of,
> Kelly of Kelly and Sheats.

ALUM: Oh yes, your sense of humor. Get rid of it.

MARTINAS: My poem?

ALUM: Not bad.

MARTINAS: Not bad! You academic low-grade moron! Can't you say more about it?

ALUM: Not with your butcher knife on the table.

MARTINAS: What do *you* know? Charlatan, Svengali, cheapskate!

ALUM: Cheapskate?

MARTINAS: Charging so little.

ALUM: Little?

MARTINAS: Three dollars, that's all you're getting so that's all you're charging.

ALUM: It's been a pleasure hating you; learn to read, so I can write you a scathing note of thanks. You beginner!

MARTINAS: Me? Learn to read? Catch your disease? Never. Goombye, Doctor Professor.

ALUM: Take your three dollars and shove it—in an envelope and send it to Archilochus Shemasky, c/o the Home for Homeless Men.

MARTINAS: Why are you disguised as brilliant Professor Alum, philosopher, philologist, critic, and halfback for Heidelberg in '34?

ALUM: Do I look like brilliant Professor Alum?

MARTINAS: I've never seen the fool.

ALUM: I never heard of Alum. I'm a poet. Nothing more, plenty less. I came for a Santa Claus position, dispatched here by the Jeffrey Freedom Employment Agency. And I'll make a good Santa, Mr. Martinas. I've never owned anything.

MARTINAS: So you want to be a Santa? My Santas have to give away meats to the kiddies, teeny weeners, liverwurst cones, chicken feet: we call them tidbits for tots.

ALUM: Lovely.

MARTINAS: You don't mind kids yelling, grabbing for snacks, stuffing their little faces with food?

ALUM: Lovely.

MARTINAS: You're fired. Goombye. You'd give away all my profits. A man doesn't build thirty-five floors of meat by giving all his food to kiddies. First floor, loins of beef; second floor, veal; third, lamb; fourth, me, a large apartment, French provincial iceboxes, blood cocktail bar (*Drinks one himself.*); fifth floor, the various marrows . . .

ALUM: Goombye. (*Exit.*)

MARTINAS (*into intercom*): Get me the Jeffrey Freedom Employment Agency. The real Professor Alum, philosopher, philologist, critic, and halfback for Heidelberg in '34 should be here any minute. Throw him out. (*Picks up phone, talks into it.*) Jeffrey? What kind of employment agency are you running? I wanted a Santa Claus with heart, savoir-faire, gusto, and a private income. I wanted a red-blooded, red-nosed, red-cheeked, red-flanneled man for the job.

What did you send me? A red. A bolshevik. And if I wanted to get him in trouble I'd call him a Communist, the commie. Goombye!

Enter WILMER *and* BEZ. BEZ *sits on the chopping table-desk and begins tearing a doll apart as* MARTINAS *looks over two Santa masks and puts them aside together.*

WILMER (*having climbed thirty-five flights*): Thirty-five floors of meat, what a marvel!

MARTINAS: Stop criticizing! Haven't I seen you before? What qualifies you as beloved Santa Claus of the Martinas Meat Mart?

WILMER: I used to make and sell dolls. Dolls were the key.

BEZ *chops doll with meat cleaver.* WILMER *faints.*

MARTINAS (*helps* BEZ *revive* WILMER): What happened?

WILMER (*takes tidbit from a Santa Claus bag*): The smell! I'm starving. (*Eats.*) This is the best tidbit for tots I've ever had.

MARTINAS: I'm glad. Stop eating. You're on my time.

WILMER: I'm in?

MARTINAS: Put on this Santa Claus mask and hat. I had another mask somewhere, younger looking.

WILMER *puts on mask and hat; tries to steal a tidbit, but* BEZ *slaps it out of his hand. Santa mask is fully adjusted.*

MARTINAS (*indicates* WILMER'S *masked face*): Bez, my son, what do you think? Where's the other mask? Did he eat it?

BEZ: Let's hear him laugh.

WILMER *sobs behind mask.*

Beautiful. He'll make an authentic Santa.

MARTINAS (*giving rest of uniform to* WILMER): You're in!
Put on the rest of the uniform.

WILMER (*weeping, arms outstretched*): Bez, my Bez—

MARTINAS: Oh Santa, you're on *my* time.

BEZ: He should double the gross intake this week, Dad.

WILMER *puts on Santa uniform.*

MARTINAS: Bez can't read, but he sure can count!

WILMER: Please, may I hear him count.

MARTINAS: Count, Bez, my child.

BEZ: One, two, three, three-fifty, four, four and a
quarter . . .

MARTINAS: Add?

BEZ: One chop plus one chop is two chops. Dad, what an
advertising stunt. The Santa scheme cost fifty dollars
tops, but it should net us somewhere in the neighborhood of—

WILMER *has finished changing into Santa uniform;*
BEZ *sees* WILMER *as Santa and rushes into his arms.*

Santa! Santa! (*Sits on* WILMER's *lap.*) What am I
going to get for Christmas?

WILMER: I don't know. Does that qualify me as a non-
Santa? O Bez, Bez . . .

BEZ *leaps off* WILMER's *lap.* WILMER *reaches out,*

weeping, one hand toward BEZ, *one hand toward the food.*

MARTINAS: Bez, did you see my other Santa Claus mask? I had them both together. (*Looking for mask.*) Hey, what's this filthy suitcase?

BEZ: Some bum gave it to me.

WILMER *sobs.*

MARTINAS: You're on *my* time, Santa. Now get out there and give! (*Gives* WILMER *bag of tidbits.*)

WILMER *is about to leave.*

Wait! One question.

WILMER: Yes?

MARTINAS: What am I going to get for Christmas?

Blackout.

SCENE THREE

The street.

WILMER *in Santa uniform leaves* MARTINAS' *building, calls to passers-by laden with Christmas packages and dressed as if they themselves were gift-wrapped.*

WILMER: Tidbits for tots! Compliments of the O. O. Martinas Meat Mart. Bring them home to the kiddies. Candied sweetbreads, chocolate covered tripe, chicken feet.

SELMA *approaches. She is wearing a suit that looks as if it is made of Christmas wrapping of silk and silver.*

WILMER's *Santa mask expresses shock, then grief.* SELMA *walks to him and* WILMER *joyfully opens his arms.*

SELMA: Uniform's too big. I'll speak to O. O. about it.

WILMER: Don't you know me?

SELMA: Of course. You're Santa Claus. Merry Christmas. That uniform makes you pathetic and poor, Santa. Anyone would think you're a bum.

She goes toward building.

WILMER: Selma . . .

SELMA: Someone calls.

Romantic music.

WILMER: Selma!

SELMA: A voice I've known.

WILMER *rushes to her and triumphantly takes off his mask. Beneath it is the other Santa Claus mask.*

WILMER: Selma!

SELMA: I was right. You *are* Santa Claus.

WILMER *tries to take other mask off.* SELMA *helps him and when she sees his face, she weeps.*

WILMER: Yes, it's Wilmer Flange, your former casual acquaintance and husband.

SELMA: You don't look well. Have you failed in your several chosen fields?

WILMER: I'm all right. I'll be a traveling Santa. The key? America in the winter: Argentina in the summer. Santas down there don't have the old American know-how. I'll be in demand. I'll be loved. And in Spanish. Come with me.

SELMA: I'm O.K. with O. O.

WILMER: Some men would weep and plead and beg. Me, I'm one of them. Come back to me, Selma. Finally realized you're my type.

SELMA: Kiss me.

WILMER: On the street?

SELMA: On the mouth.

They kiss.

WILMER: I knew it! I knew you knew I really knew we were really the type for each other. I knew you hated that ignorant old man, knew you didn't need him, him when you had me, me.

SELMA: Yes, yes! Kiss. Kiss.

They kiss, kiss. Music stops.

And now good-by. I realize I said I'll be waiting whenever you need me, so I hope there are no hard feelings that I've grown used to O. O. Beneath that crude exterior lies a pot of gold. And I need money for when I become rich. I'll thank you not to call him an ignorant old, useless old, impotent old man.

WILMER: I didn't say he was impotent.

SELMA: Yes, well, anyway. Don't you see, Wilmer, life isn't everything. (*Exit.*)

WILMER: If ever you need me, Selma—

WILMER *puts on one Santa Claus mask and holds the*

other in his hands. Gloom settles around him, but a ray of light picks out still another bearded—though thinner—Santa face.

WILMER: A fellow Santa! If I can't have love, I want companionship.

The other Santa steps into the light and is revealed as no Santa at all. He is UNCLE SAM. *He points at* WILMER *as in the famous poster.*

UNCLE SAM: I want you!

UNCLE SAM *helps* WILMER *into army uniform from Santa uniform and* WILMER *marches off with rifle.*

Blackout.

SCENE FOUR

PROJECTION ON CURTAIN

"WAR"

The slide is cracked to give the impression of barbed wire. Another projection follows: An exclamation point all by itself.

A battlefield. Night. WILMER *is advancing, rifle in hand. Battle noises, smoke. Occasional flares. Other soldiers are dimly seen in the background.*

FIRST SOLDIER: Do we advance?

WILMER: I don't know.

SECOND SOLDIER: Where are we heading?

WILMER: I don't know.

THIRD SOLDIER: What will we do after we get there?

WILMER: I don't know.

FIRST SOLDIER: Say, who are you?

WILMER: I'm in Central Intelligence.

SECOND SOLDIER: *Let's retreat!*

ALL: Swell!

THIRD SOLDIER (*to* SECOND SOLDIER): Which way is back?

WILMER: I don't know.

> *Three soldiers exit in confusion, bumping into each other as they go. Left alone,* WILMER *shrugs his shoulders. The flares have died out and the stage is completely black.*
>
> *After a few moments, the glow of a lighted cigarette becomes visible on one side of the stage.*
>
> WILMER, *unseen, moves toward the lighted cigarette.*

WILMER: I beg your pardon. Could I bother you for a cigarette?

Silence.

Got a light?

WILMER *takes a light from the other cigarette.*

I'm tired of being drafted. I didn't mind those two wars last year, but now I'm highly involved in a project which leaves me no time for war—namely: military history. I believe in history. It's the key, you know. For example, people learn from military history how to avoid war. Think of the chaos the world would be in today if it had no military history. My motto is: Be nice to history and history will enjoy you.

Other soldier snores.

WILMER: Don't fall asleep. Please.

Bomb falls.

It's dangerous while smoking.

ENEMY SOLDIER (*in thick German accent*): Shh! A zoldier cannot zome zleep around here get?

WILMER: Where did you get that accent?

ENEMY SOLDIER: Oxford.

WILMER: That's a German accent. Are you of German descent?

ENEMY SOLDIER: Ja vohl.

WILMER: You're not my enemy by any chance?

ENEMY SOLDIER: Ja vohl.

WILMER: Wilmer Flange is the name. Happy to meet one of you. I like your work. I admire your military strategy.

Bomb explodes with enormous noise. Livid green light takes the stage.

ENEMY SOLDIER:

In the light he is seen to be a bucktoothed, wild-looking Japanese soldier with sword.

Vat a boom!

WILMER: No offense, but you're very Japanese.

ENEMY SOLDIER: Only on mein father's side. Mom vas

German.

WILMER: Must we fight each other to the death?

ENEMY SOLDIER: Zilence! The enemy will hear.

WILMER: The enemy?

ENEMY SOLDIER: Our superior officers.

WILMER: Are you like me? A pacifist fighting to end war?

ENEMY SOLDIER: Ja vohl. I was shot in the head and driven sane.

WILMER: Sorry. Hope I didn't do it.

ENEMY SOLDIER: Today for surgery I'm leaving.

WILMER: Tokyo?

ENEMY SOLDIER: Nein.

WILMER: Berlin?

ENEMY SOLDIER: Nein.

WILMER: Boston? Ha ha ha—

ENEMY SOLDIER: Nein. New York. I go now to dem dere United States. I have a psychiatrist uncle in the Vest Eighties.

WILMER: You're going to America? Selma lives there, the former mother of my ex-wife's child, Bez. (*Taking out pencil and paper.*) Give her this note to remind her to miss me. I haven't seen her in many a war. (*Writing.*) If ever you need me, I'll be waiting . . .

ENEMY SOLDIER: I must go!

WILMER: Here!

Hands him letter. ENEMY SOLDIER *swallows it.*

ENEMY SOLDIER (*leaving*): It's been a pleasure. Auf-wiedersehn.

WILMER (*waving*): Banzai. Here's hoping we see each other again—maybe through a pair of binoculars.

A blast. Exit ENEMY SOLDIER *who takes* WILMER'S *rifle by mistake.*

WILMER (*holding sword*): Another shot heard round the world.

Blackout.

SCENE FIVE

PROJECTION ON CURTAIN

"MORE WAR"

Another projection follows: Two exclamation points by themselves.

The street. Years later. Shoeshine stand. Night.

FIRST POLICEMAN: War!

SECOND POLICEMAN: The wars roll by like cherry pits down the City Hall steps.

Talking to man shining his shoes, who is in the shadows, back to audience.

The cows hanging in the O. O. Martinas window upside down see nothing but marching shoes war after war after war.

FIRST POLICEMAN: I don't like animals to see me upside

down. I look funny upside down. My smile looks too sad, and my sad looks too smile, my feet look too head and my head looks too dead. This is a depressing war.

SECOND POLICEMAN: It's a fun war for some. O. O. has the joy of donating to soldiers juicy, fat steaks under that juicy, fat government contract.

FIRST POLICEMAN: A dollar-a-year man.

SECOND POLICEMAN: A dollar-a-pound man. Little wonder he was made honorary President of the United States.

FIRST POLICEMAN: Another six stories added to the building. Young Bez grown older, a chip off the old chopping block, graduated from sculpture school with a B.C.—Bachelor of Carving, now an airborne army butcher.

SECOND POLICEMAN: While his former dad, Wilmer—

FIRST POLICEMAN: A mere private, slowly rising to the rank of conscientious objector.

SECOND POLICEMAN: Wilmer always was conscientious.

FIRST POLICEMAN: Let's not talk about the war.

SECOND POLICEMAN: You're right. War troubles trouble me.

FIRST POLICEMAN: That doesn't sound like you, André.

SECOND POLICEMAN: Nowadays people do everything they don't want. It was better before the war when they had no more money. Now they have more money. That's why they have to rob to keep up their standard of living. Look, for instance. There's a robber robbing.

A man is robbed by HIGH HAT ROBBER. SECOND POLICEMAN *draws gun,* ROBBER *shoots first and runs off.* SECOND POLICEMAN *holds his heart, falls to the ground.* FIRST POLICEMAN *and robbery* VICTIM *rush to* SECOND POLICEMAN'S *aid.*

SECOND POLICEMAN: I'm done.

FIRST POLICEMAN: André, André! Your life's not done.

SECOND POLICEMAN (*jumps up healthily*): Not my life. My career as a policeman. I'm retiring from the force.

FIRST POLICEMAN: Weren't you shot?

SECOND POLICEMAN: No. I made believe so he would run away scared and never shoot again. He didn't mean to be mean. The war made him nervous.

FIRST POLICEMAN: Now that you're retiring from the force, maybe we can become partners in the music business. And . . .

They tiptoe off into darkness. Both snapping their fingers in rhythm. The VICTIM *watches and wonders.*

The HIGH HAT ROBBER *is advancing on him from behind, gun in hand, as stage darkens to blackout.*

SCENE SIX

MARTINAS *apartment. Years later.* MARTINAS *sits at one of his chopping tables: He eats a rapid meal of six meat courses, each separately announced and served by* SELMA, *in a negligee.*

SELMA: Hummingbirds stuffed with condor livers; ham

sandwich on pork; filet mignon wrapped in filet mignon; lamb chop aspic; artichokes made of veal; and a nice glass of gravy to wash it down. For dessert, goose mousse.

MARTINAS: What a wonderful breakfast!

SELMA: You deserve it darling after your war effort—contributing meat and keeping it at ceiling price.

MARTINAS: What a wonderful summery winter's day. Let's go to the park and have brunch. Make a basketful of stew . Unch. Unch. Nice word, "Brunch." Sounds like a combination of two words. "Unch" for lunch and "Br" for brunch. (*Cute as he can be.*) Unch, Unch, I think it comes from the Gaelic. Uncho, unchere, unchui, unctuous.

SELMA: That's Greek.

MARTINAS (*picking his teeth*): Gaelic. I know: I had a Dutch uncle. Corned beef's in my cavity from last night.

SELMA: We had bunny last night.

MARTINAS: We had corned beef. Proof? We had eagle on the side. We always have eagle with corned beef.

SELMA: It was not eagle, it was pigeon, with bunny.

> *Doorbell rings.* SELMA *opens door.* ENEMY SOLDIER *appears. Draws* WILMER's *letter out of his mouth like long piece of string.* MARTINAS *tips him.* ENEMY SOLDIER *exits bowing.*

MARTINAS: I've been in butchery all my life. Eagle goes with corned beef.

> SELMA *reads the note, then her romantic music is*

heard. Folds note carefully and puts it next to her heart.

SELMA: Prove it!

MARTINAS: I can take you to the library.

SELMA: Take me to a movie. Let's go see "Das Kapital" by Marx.

MARTINAS: I can't stand comics.

SELMA: Then let's go see "The Critique of Pure Reason."

MARTINAS: Saw it.

SELMA: Me too, but I only remember what I said about it: Melville's worst book.

MARTINAS: A good writer, for good readers.

SELMA: *I'm* a bad reader? You can't even read badly!

MARTINAS: Aristotle always said all things find their natural place in the order of things. Good writers, good readers: bad writers—

SELMA: If all things found their natural place in the order of things, my fist would find your eye.

MARTINAS: We can't even have a decent argument. Selma, the old thrill's gone. What's happened to our setup?

SELMA: I don't like critics who can't read.

MARTINAS: I go to the movies.

SELMA (*angry again*): Who cares? Stubborn fool!

There is a tremendous noise and the whole apartment shakes.

MARTINAS: My God! What is that implosion?

CRASH, and they rush to each other's arms.

SELMA: The end of the world. I know it. Oh, dearest of all butchers, hold me tight. Carry me gently to hell. (*Sobs.*)

MARTINAS: Darling, you're not going to hell: you're intelligent.

SELMA: I'm not a well-informed person.

MARTINAS: You're fairly well read.

Another BOOM.

Before we die, one thing—recite my last poem.

They hold each other desperately as SELMA *recites.*

SELMA: Love is like a red red eye,
            It makes you cry to see it.
            Love is a bloodshot eye,
            It hurts too much to cry back.
            Love is like a red red eye,
            It makes your eye red when you see it.
            Love is like an alcoholic eye,
            It makes you ashamed it can see you.
            Love is like a red, red eye
            Red eyeballs, red eyelids, red eyelobes,
                                    red brain lobes
            A very red, very stormy eye.

The shaking of the house has been gradually subsiding. When it stops at last SELMA *and* MARTINAS *look unbelieving at the wonderful world still there.*

SELMA: Darling, what happened? Did you hear that boom?

MARTINAS: Sweetie, let's listen to the radio. Find out what happened. By the way, it was an implosion, not a boom.

SELMA: A boom! Probably a bomb, darling.

MARTINAS (*goes to radio*): It was an implosion caused by the weather, sweetie.

SELMA: I think no. (*Turns on radio.*)

RADIO: Authorities have not determined if the implosion was another shot heard round the world—the bomb to end all booms—, or if the boom was based on the weather—, or if the weather which caused the implosion was caused by the boom of the bomb—, or whether the weather—

MARTINAS (*turns off radio*): See?

SELMA: See what, sweetie? He called it a boom. Bombs cause booms.

MARTINAS: Darling, he said the weather. Ergo: implosion.

SELMA: What do you know about the weather?

MARTINAS: I may not know much about the weather, but I know what I like.

SELMA (*yells*): Don't yell at me! It was a boom.

MARTINAS (*yells*): Implosion! I - M - P - L - N - X - R. Implosion!

SELMA *starts toward door.*

MARTINAS: Goombye!

SELMA: *Boom*bye!

SELMA *rushes out putting coat over her negligee. She slams the door behind her.*

Blackout.

SCENE SEVEN

Restaurant. High upright piano is being played: back of piano faces audience. No pianist is visible.

WILMER (*enters in civilian clothes brushing debris from shoulder*): What sweet music. It should be played on a harpsichord.

Piano bumps him in consternation.

No offense, but pianos simply don't have that old-world swing.

Piano bumps him again and starts to leave.

What did I do? Please talk to me.

Piano keeps moving slowly away.

I haven't spoken to anyone in ages. Since my discharge I don't get around much. My life's work occupies my life: musicology, it's all I have. My friends are dead or married. I married a few days ago. A lady and a musician. What more could a man ask for? She had no children, no parents. No technique. We were divorced this morning.

Piano moves sympathetically toward him.

Can you find it in your hands to forgive me for criticizing?

Piano takes pity, starts to play.

Maybe not a harpsichord after all; a clavichord.

The piano moves off-stage in disgust leaving WILMER *abandoned.*

SELMA *in coat over negligee rushes in.*

SELMA: I'm glad the first place I looked I found you.

WILMER: Selma Chargesse, casual acquaintance and wife —but whose?

SELMA: Didn't you hear the big boom?

WILMER: Yes. E flat. Heard it passing a movie. The theater caved in.

SELMA: What was playing?

WILMER: Too sad to remember.

SELMA: Saw it. What caused the boom? Bomb or weather?

WILMER (*warily*): Which do you think?

MARTINAS *appears in doorway, in same clothes as previous scene, arms spread-eagled.*

SELMA: Bomb.

WILMER: Yes—bomb.

SELMA: Darling! We *are* each other's type!

WILMER: Selma, I need *you*, more than Beethoven's Piano Sonata Number 32 in C Minor, Opus 111, composed at Mödling in the summer of 1820.

They embrace.

MARTINAS (*rushes in, throws an arm warmly around each*): We're all each other's types. I too say it was a bomb. By the way Selma Chargesse meet Wilmer Flange. I've been wanting to get you kids together for a long time. (*Sweet.*) Kids, listen to an old illiterate (*Angry and smug.*) who's done pretty well for himself in a world of misjudgment, misconception, mismanagement, Miss America—and misplosions. (*Sweetly.*) We three need one another like holes in the head—need patches. We can be partners in the

O. O. Martinas All American, All Meat Mart. Forty-eight stories, but growing, a big silver and stucco ever-growing soul. What do you say, kids? Let's spend the rest of our lives together just for the fun of it. Haven't I seen you somewhere?

WILMER (*to* MARTINAS): Partners? Would you turn around while we decide?

MARTINAS *turns, but stays in the same spot, a foot away, eavesdropping.*

WILMER: Selma, maybe we should. You spend so much time running back to O. O., I'd see more of you if I ran with you. The only time you need me is when you're with him.

SELMA: It was only the money of it.

WILMER: What money? It was the bleeding animal flesh of it. The meat of it.

SELMA: You mean meat might be the key?

WILMER: I mean ...

WILMER *and* SELMA (*together*): We mean meat is the key. We mean we *are* all one another's types. We mean— O.K., O. O.

MARTINAS: Thank you, children. What was your verdict?

WILMER *and* SELMA (*together*): We'll spend the rest of our lives with you.

All three march off.

Enter piano playing, back to audience. Piano stops.

SECOND POLICEMAN *appears from behind piano.*

SECOND POLICEMAN: Glad I retired from the force and took up piano?

FIRST POLICEMAN (*appears from behind piano*): Glad I retired from the force and took up page turning? André, don't they remind you of the three people who used to be around here always laughing and in trouble?

SECOND POLICEMAN: They cannot be the same. They haven't changed enough.

Curtain.

SCENE EIGHT

PROJECTION ON CURTAIN

Years later:
"The Ending: In which it all Begins."

Years later. MARTINAS *and* SELMA *behind the three chopping tables, cutting meat.* WILMER *enters guiltily with a towel wrapped around one hand, carrying a meat cleaver in his other hand.* WILMER *and* SELMA *are middle-aged;* MARTINAS *hasn't changed. Three huge sides of beef behind them, engulfing them.*

SELMA: Wilmer, you've cut yourself again.

MARTINAS (*unwraps towel and looks at the bloody wound*): How can you keep cutting your hand after ten years in the business?

WILMER: I was juggling cleavers in the refrigerator to keep warm. I read in a magazine I wrap sweetbreads in that the Navaho country is warm.

MARTINAS: He's too human for a human.

WILMER: You know what I want? To live way out there among the Navaho.

MARTINAS: Back to work. We've got the biggest order of our career: two tons of corned beef, two tons of roast beef, six miles of frankfurters and a sprinkling of chicken livers. Becount of they're having a party.

WILMER: Why weren't we invited?

MARTINAS: They say we're not as good as the next fellow. Selma, take over the corned beef.

SELMA: Righto, O. O.

MARTINAS: Wilmer, step up production on the roast beef.

WILMER: Righto, O. O.

MARTINAS: O. O. cover the knockwurst. Righto, O. O.

They all resume their work, cutting and cleaving meat in silence. Music.

WILMER: Selma, if you love me, come! I want to live way out there among the Navaho.

SELMA: Too old to begin a new life. Look at the girl you wooed and won years and years ago. Weak, tired. Not the gay slip of a thing I used to be—beautiful, agile, able, hopeful, and a swell dancer. How can I live way out there among the Navaho?

WILMER: I've read that the Navaho life is different.

SELMA: Your bursitis, your arthritis, your bronchitis, your

corns. Dearest butcher . . .

WILMER: I want to learn ancestral customs, primitive dances. I want to make sand paintings and rugs to send my friends on Christmas and the Fourth of July and Independence Day. O. O., tell her you'll send us our fair share of the Mart each month.

MARTINAS: You know I cheat. Oh, just a little, mind you: take advantage in a small harmless way. Sort of cute, you see (*Suddenly violent.*), the world can't kick me around, O. O. The world better watch out, O. O., or I take it between these two fingers and squeeze it like a louse, O. O.

   WILMER *and* SELMA *rush to their work.*

   (*Sweetly.*) No, I like Wilmer near me! I don't want him way out there among the Navaho.

SELMA: Wilmer, I've always loved you, I love you still. I'll love you when I'm old, when it's difficult to love anyone or anything but the proper function of the bodily functions. I'll love you a long time after we're dead . . . but—

WILMER: The Navaho still worship the good old gods, I hear tell. They do not kneel before new shrines, they are not blinded by the glitter of new shrines.

MARTINAS: All that glitters is not new shrines.

   They resume rhythmic cutting and cleaving. WOMAN *and her small son enter.*

WOMAN: Pound of lovers, please.

MARTINAS: You mean livers, Madam?

WOMAN: Didn't I say livers?

MARTINAS: You said lovers.

WOMAN: Perhaps I said loivers. The word loivers is closer to livers than lovers. (*To* BOY.) Don't you think so, Wilmer?

BOY: Yarths.

WILMER: What?

BOY: Yarths.

WILMER: I mean "What! Is his name Wilmer?"

BOY: Yarths. Mother of mothers, I've changed my mind. Phonetically speaking, the similarity between the words "Loivers" and "Livers" cannot be denied. However, "Lovers" is closer to "Livers" because both words have meanings, whereas "Loivers" and "Livers" have no such kinship. Do you understand, lady of ladies?

WOMAN: Yes. Shut up.

MARTINAS: What a brilliant butcher he'd make. Like our former son, Bez, the first Astro-butcher, lost in orbit.

They bow their heads in a moment of silent tribute.

WILMER (*exits, returns with package of livers*): Your livers!

WOMAN: For my cat, Wilmer.

MARTINAS: How did you know my friend's name was Wilmer?

WOMAN: I was talking about my cat, Wilmer. It's for him I buy lovers. (*To* BOY.) Right, Wilmer? I mean about our cat, Wilmer, Wilmer.

BOY: Yarths.

MARTINAS: Wait, Wilmer, say yes!

BOY: Yarths.

MARTINAS: Say no.

BOY: No.

MARTINAS: My proof worked. He says yarths instead of yes.

BOY: Only when I express the affirmative. Yarths, dear of dears?

WOMAN: Yes, you have a mind. Shut up.

BOY: Yarths.

WILMER: One question.

MARTINAS: How can I resist? Wilmer's like a lump of gold in this black night of our day.

WILMER: The Navaho . . . ?

MARTINAS: I resist. Your idea is simply not as good as other ideas I've come across. "What goes up must come down." There's *my* idea of an idea.

BOY: Yarths?

WILMER (*to* WOMAN): Why does he say yarths? He has such a nice command of other words.

WOMAN: A lovely command.

MARTINAS: One of the loveliest commands I, personally, have come across. And I've come across quite a few commands in my day.

WILMER: I, personally, have come across very few commands. I have not seen much of these United States. For instance, I want to live way out there among the Navaho, a fine folk in the field of the rug and the pot.

BOY: Fine trinkets too: fine silverwork, fine beads, and they worship the good old gods.

WILMER: You—?

BOY: Yarths, I've lived way out there among the Navaho. Yarths, me and dove of doves.

WOMAN: Yes. Shut up.

WILMER: Before you shut up, Wilmer . . .

BOY: Yarths, Wilmer?

WILMER: What was it like way out there among the Navaho?

BOY: Fine. Chilly at night. Yarths, heart of hearts?

WOMAN (*taking bag of livers*): Let's go feed our cat, Wilmer.

WILMER: Which Wilmer did you mean?

WOMAN: Wouldn't *you* like to go fishing in my soul of souls?

BOY: Can't we stay? I like these people. I'm sick of intelligent and charming people.

WOMAN: No, they're not as good as the next fellow.

BOY: Who is?

WOMAN: What are you thinking about?

BOY: "What goes up must come down"; smoke goes up and forgets to come down. Like you when you have the blues. When you jump out the window, the way you always promise, will you forget to come down too?

WOMAN: I hope so: I don't want to die. Shut up.

BOY: Yarths, mother of mothers, lady of ladies, dear of dears, dove of doves, heart of hearts, big fat witch!

They leave and WILMER, SELMA *and* MARTINAS *cut and chop in silence. Suddenly* WILMER *takes money from cash register, chops it with cleaver.*

WILMER: Selma, why do you hack away at bleeding flesh? Why don't you come with me to live way out there among the Navaho, mother of mothers?

SELMA: And?

WILMER (*cautiously*): Lady of ladies.

SELMA: And?

WILMER: Dear of dears?

SELMA: And?

WILMER: Heart of hearts? Dove of Doves?

SELMA: Righto! And? Big fat what?

WILMER: You're not fat. Hey, Selma! Coming to live with me way out there among the Navaho?

SELMA: Yarths!

SELMA *and* WILMER *mark time, ready to march off.*

MARTINAS (*sadly chopping meat*): Take me with you? I'll miss us three, the joy of enterprise troubles, the fun of raising a forty-nine story meat mart. Take me with you.

WILMER: Oh, no you don't talk us into another passage of history with you.

MARTINAS: I'm sick of this life, too. Not being as good as the next fellow, day in, day out. A business where all is butchery. World! Would you like a leg to eat? Not from my hands will you buy bleeding animal flesh for dollars. (*Stares at meat contritely*.) Forgive me. (*Turns to* WILMER.) Take me with you? Maybe I'll forget you taught me how to read and write and I'll build poems once more.

WILMER: Will you give up the sale of bleeding animal flesh?

MARTINAS: I am. I will. I have.

WILMER: Am what?

MARTINAS: Am giving up the sale of meat.

WILMER: Will what?

MARTINAS: Will giving it up. Have what?

WILMER: Have been feeling older since I've grown older.

SELMA: What are we getting so old about?

MARTINAS: Take me with you?

WILMER: How do we know you won't drag us back into the meat business?

MARTINAS: Becount of I'm going into—the fish business, where I can live and be free. I belong in the fish business. It's what I've always wanted in my head of heads. Tomorrow we go way out there among the Navaho. The Navaho, where I buy my dream fish department store, fifty floors of fish. First floor, flounder; second floor, sea bass; third floor, blubber; fourth floor, me, a large apartment, but the finest Navaho rugs and sand paintings; fifth floor, sea weed . . .

As they all march off.

Curtain.

Wilmer and Selma

Vendor and Wilmer

Martinas and Waitress

Selma and Wilmer

First and Second Policeman with High Hat Robber and Victim

Wilmer's toy invention studio

Enemy Soldier and Wilmer

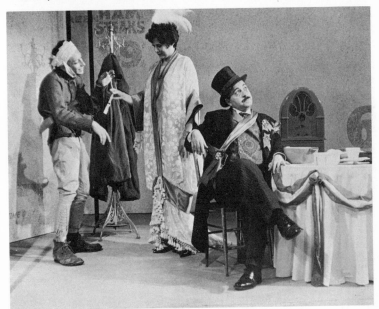

The O.O. Martinas apartment

The O.O. Martinas Meat Department Store

Selma, Martinas, and Wilmer